How To Survive

UNBEARABLE STRESS

Second Edition

WITHDRAWN *27x(1/11)* *5/12*

By
Steven L. Burns, M.D.

26x(1/09) *6/10*

19 x 6/06 ✓ 1/07

illustrated by: Kimberley Burns

18x 3/06

17x7/04

13x 9/01 ✓ 9/02

I-MED PRESS

✓3/03

ACKNOWLEDGEMENT

This book is the product of six years of discussions, research and clinical practice by myself and Wayne Nickens, M.D., C.A.C. Many of the ideas that we began developing together have come to fruition in this work. I am sorry that Dr. Nickens was not available to co-author this book, but other commitments prevented him from doing so.

Portions of the material in this book have been derived from my writings in NOT GUILTY/NOT CRAZY, a work by myself and Dr. Nickens, concerning the physiology and treatment of alcoholism. This book was privately printed for use in our medical practices and educational endeavors.

The "Stress Scales" used in this book were provided to me by the Foundation for National Education on Alcoholism and Drug Abuse (a non-profit educational foundation). They are modifications of the "Social Readjustment Rating Scale" by Thomas Holmes and Richard Rahe. This scale was first published in the "Journal of Psychosomatic Research", Copyright 1967, vol.11 p.214. It is used by permission of Pergamon Press Ltd.

I would like to thank my wife, Kimberley, for her encouragement during times when this project faltered, and for the many hours she has spent editing and illustrating this work.

Steve Burns, M.D.

Published by the I-MED Press
P.O. Box 3747, Huntington Beach, California 92605-3747
Manufactured in the United States of America
Typesetting and indexing by The Image Set, Santa Ana, California
ISBN 0-933131-02-X

CONTENTS

1

Recognizing
Stress

RECOGNIZING STRESS

Which of these is stress?

- ☐ You receive a promotion at work.
- ☐ Your car has a flat tire.
- ☐ You go to a fun party that lasts till 2:00 a.m.
- ☐ Your dog gets sick.
- ☐ Your new bedroom set is being delivered.
- ☐ Your best friend and his wife come to stay at your house for a week.
- ☐ You get a bad case of hay fever.
- ☐ All of the above.

ALL OF THESE ARE STRESS

If you are used to thinking that stress is something that makes you worry, you have the wrong idea of stress. Stress is many different kinds of things: happy things, sad things, allergic things, physical things. Many people carry enormous stress loads and they do not even realize it!

WHAT IS STRESS?

We are all familiar with the word "stress". Stress is when you are worried about getting laid off your job, or worried about having enough money to pay your bills, or worried about your mother when the doctor says she may need an operation. In fact, to most of us, stress is synonymous with worry. If it is something that makes you worry, then it is stress.

Your body, however, has a much broader definition of stress. TO YOUR BODY, STRESS IS ANYTHING THAT CAUSES CHANGE. It doesn't matter if it is a "good" change, or a "bad" change, they are both stress. If you break up with your boyfriend, that is stress. When you get back together again, that is stress. If your landlord sells your apartment and you have to move, that is stress. When you find your dream apartment and get ready to move, that is stress. Good or bad, if it is a CHANGE in your life, it is stress as far as your body is concerned.

Even IMAGINED CHANGE is stress. (Imagining changes is what we call "worrying".) If you fear that you will not have enough money to pay your rent, that is stress. If you worry that you may get fired, that is stress. If you think that you may receive a promotion at work, that is also stress (even though this would be a good change). Whether the event is good or bad, imagining changes in your life is stressful.

Anything that causes CHANGE IN YOUR DAILY ROUTINE is stressful.

Anything that causes CHANGE IN YOUR BODY HEALTH is stressful.

IMAGINED CHANGES are just as stressful as real changes.

Let us look at several types of stress – – ones that are so commonplace that you might not even realize that they are stressful. . . . . .

Emotional Stress

When arguments, disagreements, and conflicts cause CHANGES in your personal life – – that is stress.

Illness

Catching a cold, breaking an arm, a skin infection, a sore back, are all CHANGES in your body condition.

Pushing Your Body Too Hard

A major source of stress is overdriving yourself. If you are working (or partying) 16 hours a day, you will have reduced your available time for rest. Sooner or later, the energy drain on your system will cause the body to fall behind in its repair work. There will not be enough time or energy for the body to fix broken cells, or replace used up chemicals. CHANGES will occur in your body's internal environment. You will "hit the wall," "run out of gas". If you continue, permanent damage may be done. The body's fight to stay healthy in the face of the increased energy that you are expending is major stress.

Environmental Factors

Very hot or very cold climates can be stressful. Very high altitude may be a stress. Toxins or poisons are a stress. Each of these factors threatens to cause CHANGES in your body's internal environment.

The Special Case of Tobacco Use

Tobacco is a powerful toxin!! Smoking destroys cells that clean your trachea, bronchi, and lungs. Smoking causes emphysema and chronic bronchitis, which progress to slow suffocation. The carbon monoxide from cigarette smoking causes chronic carbon monoxide poisoning. Tobacco use damages the arteries in your body, causing insufficient blood supply to the brain, heart, and vital organs. Cigarette smoking increases the risk of cancer 50 fold.

Chewing tobacco or snuff is no safe haven. It also damages your arteries, and it carries the same cancer risk (cancers of the head and neck are particularly vicious, disfiguring, and deadly).

Poisoning the body with carbon monoxide, and causing the physical illnesses of emphysema, chronic bronchitis, cancer, and arterial damage, tobacco is a powerful source of added stress to one's life.

Hormonal Factors

PUBERTY

The vast hormonal changes of puberty are severe stressors. A person's body actually CHANGES shape, sexual organs begin to function, new hormones are released in large quantities. Puberty, as we all know, is very stressful.

PRE-MENSTRUAL SYNDROME

Once a woman passes puberty, her body is designed to function best in the presence of female hormones. For women past puberty, a lack of female hormones is a major stress on the body. Once a month, just prior to menstruation, a women's hormone levels drop sharply. In many women, the stress of sharply falling hormones is enough to create a temporary OVERSTRESS. This temporary OVERSTRESS is popularly known as Pre-Menstrual Syndrome (PMS).

POST-PARTUM

Following a pregnancy, hormone levels CHANGE dramatically. After a normal childbirth, or a miscarriage, some women may be thrown into OVERSTRESS by loss of the hormones of pregnancy.

MENOPAUSE

There is another time in a women's life when hormone levels decline. This is the menopause. The decline in hormones during menopause is slow and steady. Nevertheless, this menopausal decline causes enough stress on the body to produce OVERSTRESS in many women.

Taking Responsibility for Another Person's actions

★★
★ *When you take responsibil-*
★ *ity for another person's ac-*
★ *tions, CHANGES occur in*
★ *your life over which you*
★ *have little or no control.*
★ *Taking responsibility for an-*
★ *other person's actions is a*
★ *major stressor.*
★★

Allergic Stress

Allergic reactions are a part of your body's natural defense mechanism. When confronted with a substance which your body considers toxic, your body will try to get rid of it, attack it, or somehow neutralize it. If it is something that lands in your nose, you might get a runny, sneezy nose; in your eyes, itchy watery red eyes; on your skin, itchy red blistery skin; if you inhale it, wheezy lungs; in a food, you may break out in itchy red hives all over your body. Allergy is a definite major stress, requiring large changes in energy expenditure on the part of your body's defense system to fight off what the body perceives as a dangerous attack by an outside toxin.

The Special Case of Food Allergy

There is much confusion in the scientific literature regarding food allergy. What we do know about food allergies is as follows: Many infants have violent reactions to certain foods. The reactions may be terrible skin rashes, colicky abdominal pain, wheezing, or bloody diarrhea. After several years, the children can usually tolerate the foods without severe reaction. They are, however, still allergic to the foods. What has happened is that the intestines and immune system have matured, and the allergic food reactions are not as violent as before. Now, the body responds with a chronic stuffy nose, a few patches of skin rash, or frequent ear infections.

The parents think the child has "out grown" his allergy, so the child continues to consume the offending food. Cow's milk is the most common offender; and children tend to consume it in very large amounts, even though it may be a constant source of allergic stress on the body. Thus, the child who is allergic to milk (or other substances) may be carrying a very large stress load at an early age. Since the child's immune system has learned to tone down the violent reactions of infant days, the allergy may only manifest itself as a chronic stuffy nose, recurrent ear infections, a few patches of skin rash, occasional allergic wheezing or itchy eyes. It is important to realize that although symptoms may appear minor, THESE MINOR SYMPTOMS MAY INDICATE A CHILD WITH A MAJOR ALLERGIC STRESS LOAD.

2

Your Stress Scale

YOUR STRESS SCALE

In the following table you can look up representative changes in your life and see how much stress value each of these changes is adding to your life. CIRCLE ANY ITEM THAT YOU MAY HAVE EXPERIENCED IN THE LAST TWELVE MONTHS. Then, total up your score.

	EVENT	STRESS VALUES
1.	DEATH OF SPOUSE	100
2.	DIVORCE	60
3.	MENOPAUSE	60
4.	SEPARATION FROM LIVING PARTNER	60
5.	JAIL TERM OR PROBATION	60
6.	DEATH OF CLOSE FAMILY MEMBER OTHER THAN SPOUSE	60
7.	SERIOUS PERSONAL INJURY OR ILLNESS	45
8.	MARRIAGE OR ESTABLISHING LIFE PARTNERSHIP	45
9.	FIRED AT WORK	45
10.	MARITAL OR RELATIONSHIP RECONCILIATION	40
11.	RETIREMENT	40
12.	CHANGE IN HEALTH OF IMMEDIATE FAMILY MEMBER	40
13.	WORK MORE THAN 40 HOURS PER WEEK	35
14.	PREGNANCY OR CAUSING PREGNANCY	35
15.	SEX DIFFICULTIES	35
16.	GAIN OF NEW FAMILY MEMBER	35
17.	BUSINESS OR WORK ROLE CHANGE	35

16

18.	CHANGE IN FINANCIAL STATE	35
19.	DEATH OF A CLOSE FRIEND (not a family member)	30
20.	CHANGE IN NUMBER OF ARGUMENTS WITH SPOUSE OR LIFE PARTNER	30
21.	MORTGAGE OR LOAN FOR A MAJOR PURPOSE	25
22.	FORECLOSURE OF MORTGAGE OR LOAN	25
23.	SLEEP LESS THAN 8 HOURS PER NIGHT	25
24.	CHANGE IN RESPONSIBILITIES AT WORK	25
25.	TROUBLE WITH IN-LAWS, OR WITH CHILDREN	25
26.	OUTSTANDING PERSONAL ACHIEVEMENT	25
27.	SPOUSE BEGINS OR STOPS WORK	20
28.	BEGIN OR END SCHOOL	20
29.	CHANGE IN LIVING CONDITIONS (visitors in the home, change in roommates, remodeling house)	20
30.	CHANGE IN PERSONAL HABITS (diet, exercise, smoking, etc.)	20
31.	CHRONIC ALLERGIES	20
32.	TROUBLE WITH BOSS	20
33.	CHANGE IN WORK HOURS OR CONDITIONS	15
34.	MOVING TO NEW RESIDENCE	15
35.	PRESENTLY IN PRE-MENSTRUAL PERIOD	15
36.	CHANGE IN SCHOOLS	15
37.	CHANGE IN RELIGIOUS ACTIVITIES	15
38.	CHANGE IN SOCIAL ACTIVITIES (more or less than before)	15
39.	MINOR FINANCIAL LOAN	10
40.	CHANGE IN FREQUENCY OF FAMILY GET-TOGETHERS	10

41.	VACATION	10
42.	PRESENTLY IN WINTER HOLIDAY SEASON	10
43.	MINOR VIOLATION OF THE LAW	5

TOTAL SCORE=_____

STRESS SCALE FOR YOUTH

EVENT		STRESS VALUES
1.	DEATH OF SPOUSE, PARENT, BOYFRIEND/GIRLFRIEND	100
2.	DIVORCE (of yourself or your parents)	65
3.	PUBERTY	65
4.	PREGNANCY (or causing pregnancy)	65
5.	MARITAL SEPARATION OR BREAKUP WITH BOYFRIEND/GIRLFRIEND	60
6.	JAIL TERM OR PROBATION	60
7.	DEATH OF OTHER FAMILY MEMBER (other than spouse, parent, boyfriend/girlfriend)	60
8.	BROKEN ENGAGEMENT	55
9.	ENGAGEMENT	50
10.	SERIOUS PERSONAL INJURY OR ILLNESS	45
11.	MARRIAGE	45
12.	ENTERING COLLEGE OR BEGINNING NEXT LEVEL OF SCHOOL (starting junior high or high school)	45
13.	CHANGE IN INDEPENDENCE OR RESPONSIBILITY	45

14.	ANY DRUG AND/OR ALCOHOL USE	45
15.	FIRED AT WORK OR EXPELLED FROM SCHOOL	45
16.	CHANGE IN ALCOHOL OR DRUG USE	45
17.	RECONCILIATION WITH MATE, FAMILY OR BOYFRIEND/GIRLFRIEND (getting back together)	40
18.	TROUBLE AT SCHOOL	40
19.	SERIOUS HEALTH PROBLEM OF FAMILY MEMBER	40
20.	WORKING WHILE ATTENDING SCHOOL	35
21.	WORKING MORE THAN 40 HOURS PER WEEK	35
22.	CHANGING COURSE OF STUDY	35
23.	CHANGE IN FREQUENCY OF DATING	35
24.	SEXUAL ADJUSTMENT PROBLEMS (confusion of sexual identity)	35
25.	GAIN OF NEW FAMILY MEMBER (new baby born or parent remarries)	35
26.	CHANGE IN WORK RESPONSIBILITIES	35
27.	CHANGE IN FINANCIAL STATE	30
28.	DEATH OF A CLOSE FRIEND (not a family member)	30
29.	CHANGE TO A DIFFERENT KIND OF WORK	30
30.	CHANGE IN NUMBER OF ARGUMENTS WITH MATE, FAMILY OR FRIENDS	30
31.	SLEEP LESS THAN 8 HOURS PER NIGHT	25
32.	TROUBLE WITH IN-LAWS OR BOYFRIEND'S OR GIRLFRIEND'S FAMILY	25
33.	OUTSTANDING PERSONAL ACHIEVEMENT (awards, grades, etc.)	25

34.	MATE OR PARENTS START OR STOP WORKING	20
35.	BEGIN OR END SCHOOL	20
36.	CHANGE IN LIVING CONDITIONS (visitors in the home, remodeling house, change in roommates)	20
37.	CHANGE IN PERSONAL HABITS (start or stop a habit like smoking or dieting)	20
38.	CHRONIC ALLERGIES	20
39.	TROUBLE WITH THE BOSS	20
40.	CHANGE IN WORK HOURS	15
41.	CHANGE IN RESIDENCE	15
42.	CHANGE TO A NEW SCHOOL (other than graduation)	15
43.	PRESENTLY IN PRE-MENSTRUAL PERIOD	15
44.	CHANGE IN RELIGIOUS ACTIVITY	15
45.	GOING IN DEBT (you or your family)	10
46.	CHANGE IN FREQUENCY OF FAMILY GATHERINGS	10
47.	VACATION	10
48.	PRESENTLY IN WINTER HOLIDAY SEASON	10
49	MINOR VIOLATION OF THE LAW	5

TOTAL SCORE=_____

We have asked you to look at the last twelve months of changes in your life. This may surprise you. It is crucial to understand, however, that a major change in your life has effects that carry over for long periods of time. It is like dropping a rock into a pond. After the initial splash, you will experience ripples of stress. And these ripples may continue in your life for at least a year.

So, if you have experienced total stress within the last twelve months of 250 or greater, even with normal stress tolerance, you may be OVERSTRESSED. Persons with Low Stress Tolerance may be OVERSTRESSED at levels as low as 150.

Carrying too heavy a stress load is like running your car engine past the red line; or leaving your toaster stuck in the "on" position; or running a nuclear reactor past maximum permissible power. Sooner or later, something will break, burn up, or melt down.

What breaks depends on where the weak links are in your physical body. And this is largely an inherited characteristic.

HERE ARE THE COMMON "WEAK LINKS"	SYMPTOMS OF MALFUNCTION
1. Brain OVERSTRESS	Fatigue, aches and pains, crying spells, depression, anxiety attacks, sleep disturbance.
2. Gastrointestinal Tract	Ulcer, cramps and diarrhea, colitis, irritable bowel.
3. Glandular System	Thyroid gland malfunction.
4. Cardiovascular	High blood pressure, heart attack, abnormal heart beat, stroke.

| 5. Skin | Itchy skin rashes. |
| 6. Immune System | Decreased resistance to infections and neoplasm. |

We have known for a long time that OVERSTRESS could cause physical damage to the gastrointestinal tract, glandular system, skin or cardiovascular system. But only recently have we learned that OVERSTRESS actually causes physical changes in the brain. One of the most exciting medical advances of our decade has been an understanding of how OVERSTRESS physically affects your brain. We now know that the fatigue, aches and pains, crying spells, depression, anxiety attacks and sleep disturbances of OVER-STRESS are caused by brain CHEMICAL MALFUNCTION.

Here is how it works...

3

Brain Chemical Messengers

BRAIN CHEMICAL MESSENGERS

The exciting discoveries began in the spring of 1977. Tools had been discovered. Tools that were enabling scientists to penetrate the very interior of single nerve cells in the brain. Important discoveries were being made almost daily about the inner workings of the brain. We now know that vital chemicals carry messages between brain cells. In essence, they allow brain cells to "talk to" one another.

On a typical day in the brain, trillions of messages are sent and received. The messages that are happy, upbeat messages are carried by the brain's "HAPPY MESSENGERS" (technically known as Biogenic Amine/Endorphin System). Other messages are somber and quieting. They are carried by the brain's "SAD MESSENGERS". Most nerve centers receive input from both types of messengers. As long as this input is balanced, everything runs along on an even keel.

Stress, however, causes problems with the brain's Happy Messengers. When life is smooth, the happy messages keep up with demand. But when too much stress is placed on the brain, the Happy Messengers begin to fall behind on their deliveries. As the stress continues, the happy messages begin to fail. Important nerve centers then receive mostly SAD MESSAGES, and the whole brain becomes distressed. The person enters a state of brain chemical imbalance known as – – OVERSTRESS.

OVERSTRESS makes people feel terrible. With SAD MESSAGES overwhelming the happy messages, a person feels "overwhelmed" by life. People complain of being tired, unable to fall asleep or to obtain a restful night's sleep. They have plagues of aches and pains, lack of energy, lack of enjoyment of life. They feel depressed, anxious, or just unable to cope with life.

25

Too many SAD messages

will cause:

Fatigue

Aches

Depression

Anxiety

Sleeplessness

Overwhelmed

Low Stress Tolerance
The Inherited Factor

Everyone inherits a certain ability to make and use Happy Messengers in the brain. As long as you can make enough Happy Messengers to keep up with the stress in your life, you will find stress to be fun, exciting, enjoyable, challenging. In fact, without it you would be bored.

However, when the amount of stress in your life is so great that you begin to run out of Happy Messengers, then bad things begin to happen. You may have sleep disturbances, aches and pains, lack of enjoyment of life and even panic attacks.

The amount of stress that you can tolerate before your Happy Messengers malfunction is referred to as your "Stress Tolerance". Your Stress Tolerance is set by your genetic inheritance.

Most of us have inherited sufficient Stress Tolerance to allow us to weather the stresses of daily living. We still feel well and enjoy life. Yet, each of us, at some time has experienced <u>short</u> periods of brain chemical imbalance.

The night you couldn't sleep before your big test at school, or your important job interview, or your "fabulous date"...

The sadness and crying you may have felt when a friend or relative passed away, or a girlfriend or boyfriend left you...

The chest pains or the headaches that you may have thought were heart problems or migraine, but your doctor said came from too much stress and strain...

We have all experienced such brief episodes of Happy Messenger malfunction. But, fully 10% of our population feels like this all of the time!

You see, one in ten persons has inherited a LOW STRESS TOLERANCE. This means that his/her Happy Messengers "poop out" at stress levels which the rest of us would consider "normal, everyday stress." The result of inheriting such a Low Stress Tolerance may be a disaster. Such a person will be operating his or her life in practically permanent OVERSTRESS. Sleep disturbances, aches and pains, fatigue, depressions, mood swings, anxiety attacks, and even drug addiction can become life long problems.

Since one in ten persons have inherited a Low Stress Tolerance, we are describing an enormous number of people.

Ten percent of your friends, your acquaintances, your employees, your co-workers, your employers... everywhere around you there are persons who are not able to cope with the stress of daily life.

To understand how stress results in this disastrous condition for so many people, let us begin by examining the brain's HAPPY MESSENGERS.

4

Three Happy Messengers

THREE HAPPY MESSENGERS

Serotonin

lets you sleep

Noradrenalin

gives you energy

Dopamine

sets your pleasure

and pain levels

THREE HAPPY MESSENGERS

There are three Happy Messengers: SEROTONIN, NORADRENALIN, and DOPAMINE. These are the brain chemicals that begin to malfunction when stress levels become more than a person can handle.

Serotonin Lets You Sleep

The Happy Messenger, Serotonin, must work properly in order for you to sleep well. Serotonin is responsible for making sure that your body's physiology is set for sleeping. If Serotonin does not do its job properly, you will not be able to obtain a restful sleep, no matter how hard you try.

Serotonin Sets Your Body Clock

Inside every one of our brains is a very accurate "Clock". This time-keeping apparatus functions like the conductor of a symphony orchestra. Just as the conductor of the orchestra keeps all the various instruments playing in rhythm, so the Body Clock keeps all the various functions of your body coordinated, and moving to the same rhythm.

The Body Clock is located deep in the center of the brain, in a little group of cells known as the Pineal Gland. Within the Pineal Gland is a store-house of the messenger Serotonin, which is the chemical "mainspring" of the Clock. Each day the Serotonin is chemically converted to a related compound, Melatonin; and then the Melatonin is converted right back to Serotonin. The whole cycle from Serotonin to Melatonin and back to Serotonin takes exactly 25 hours — and this forms your Body's Clock.

Twenty five hours? Yes, under experimental conditions of an unchanging environment, such as in a cave kept at a constant level of illumination for weeks on end, this Body Clock cycles every 25 hours. If, however, a person is exposed to a natural outdoor cycle of daylight and darkness, the Pineal Gland will automatically set itself to a 24 hour day. That is, the Pineal Gland will automatically match its cycle to the length of one Earth's day. That way, noon in the Pineal Gland is always noon on Earth. If exposed to daylight, the Pineal Gland will neither gain nor lose time, but will always cycle exactly in concert with the Earth as our planet twirls through space. The whole process of setting the Body Clock to Earth time takes about three weeks.

The 24 hour cycling of the Body Clock is important. It adjusts your body chemistry for sleeping and for waking. Every evening your Body Clock will set your physiology for sleeping; then you feel drowsy and sleep soundly. After a while, your Body Clock adjusts your physiology for waking. You then wake up and feel refreshed.

We mentioned that the Body Clock is the coordinator of your physiologic orchestra. Three important players in that orchestra are your body temperature, stress fighting hormone, and sleep cycles. Each of these must be properly coordinated by the Body Clock in order for you to sleep soundly and awake feeling rested.

The Body Clock and Your Body Temperature

Every 24 hours, your body temperature cycles from high to low, varying by as much as one degree. When it is time to wake up and be active, your body temperature rises slightly. When it is time to fall asleep, your body temperature dips slightly.

Most of us have felt how difficult it is to fall asleep on a very warm night, when you toss and turn and wish you could cool off. Contrast this with the relative comfort when one is tucked in a nice bed in a room that is slightly cool, or even downright cold. To achieve the best sleep, the body thermostat is supposed to lower slightly at night, a timing which is coordinated by your Body Clock.

The Body Clock and Your Stress Fighting Hormone

The body has a vital hormone called Cortisol, which is the body's chief stress fighting hormone. When Cortisol secretion is high, the body shifts to a "war footing". It is prepared for stress conditions such as hunger, trauma, hemorrhage, fighting, or running. Ordinarily, one's Cortisol levels will rise in the morning, as one prepares to go out into the work-a-day world. Conversely, serum Cortisol drops substantially in the evening, as one relaxes, settles down, and prepares for sleep.

As with body temperature, the ups and downs of your stress fighting hormone must cycle properly during a 24 hour day for you to achieve a restful night's sleep and awake refreshed. Any disruption of your Cortisol cycle, and restful sleep will become very difficult.

The Body Clock and Your Sleep Cycles

After falling asleep, one normally goes DEEPER and DEEPER into sleep, finally reaching a stage of deep restorative sleep. Then sleep becomes LIGHTER and LIGHTER until one enters dreaming sleep. Then the whole cycle begins over again. About every 90 minutes one goes through this cycle. In the early part of the evening the cycle pauses a relatively long time in the deepest restorative phase. As the evening progresses, the amount of time spent in deep restorative sleep lessens, and one spends more and more time dreaming. In order for one to feel rested, this sleep pattern must be cycling properly. And, of course, the cycle is regulated by your internal Body Clock.

Stress Destroys Your Sleep

The Body Clock is essential for the proper harmony of your body temperature, stress fighting hormone, and sleep cycles. In order to fall asleep easily, sleep soundly, and awake refreshed, your Body Clock must be functioning properly. The Happy Messenger, Serotonin, is the "mainspring" of the Body Clock. If stress causes Serotonin to fail, the Body Clock will stop working. You will not be able to obtain a restful sleep, no matter how hard you try.

SINCE SEROTONIN IS USUALLY THE FIRST HAPPY MESSENGER TO FAIL UNDER STRESS, THE **FIRST SIGN** *OF OVERSTRESS WILL BE INABILITY TO OBTAIN A RESTFUL SLEEP.*

When Serotonin runs low....

the Body Clock STOPS working.

The Clock has <u>STOPPED!!</u>
What do we do now?

Body-heat
Control

Sleep
Supervisor

Stress
Fighter

When the Body Clock stops working....

You CAN'T get a restful sleep.

Noradrenalin: Giving Us Energy

I am sure you have all heard of "Adrenalin". When you are frightened, Adrenalin is released into your blood stream by your adrenal glands. Your heart beats faster, blood flow is shunted away from your skin and intestines and towards your muscles. Perspiration appears on your palms and forehead. You are ready for "fight or flight". A cousin of Adrenalin, named Noradrenalin is one of the Happy Messengers. Noradrenalin has may important functions in the body's nervous system. The one that most concerns us here, however, is the role of Noradrenalin in setting your energy levels. Proper functioning of Noradrenalin in the brain is essential for you to feel energized. Without enough brain Noradrenalin you feel exhausted, tired, droopy and without energy. You just don't feel like doing anything. You just want to sit.

People with Noradrenalin failure become progressively more and more lethargic. They do not seem to have any energy to do anything. Running your brain with low Noradrenalin is akin to running your car with a failing battery. Sooner or later, it just won't start.

When Noradrenalin runs low ....

you DON'T have any energy.

Dopamine: Your Pleasure and Your Pain

As you probably know, morphine and heroin are the most potent pain relieving and pleasure producing medications known to man. They are so potent in fact, that they were long believed to mimic some unknown, but naturally occurring, body chemical. A recent technological advance has led to the remarkable uncovering of natural morphine-like molecules that are, indeed, made in each of our brains. Collectively, these substances are known as ENDORPHINS, and they are responsible for regulating our moment to moment awareness of pain.

It appears that in the discovery of Endorphins we have found our body's naturally occurring mechanism for regulating pain. It is likely that a certain baseline secretion of Endorphin occurs at all times in the body. Under certain conditions, this Endorphin secretion may rise, making the person relatively insensitive to pain. Under other conditions, the Endorphin levels may drop, making a person more sensitive than usual to pain.

Individual variations of Endorphin level would explain the observation that people may react with differing levels of perceived pain when suffering the same painful stimulus. In medical practice it is quite common to see one person with an injury have very little discomfort, while another person with a very similar injury has terrible discomfort. In the past we have said that such unusual suffering was "all in the person's head". Now we may speculate that what is different in that person's head is the Endorphin level. Hence, the person who seems to have an unusual amount of discomfort from what appears to be a trivial injury, probably is feeling more pain. For some reason, his body's own pain control mechanism has been depleted of Endorphins.

Now, our third Happy Messenger, Dopamine, seems to be concentrated in areas of the brain immediately adjacent to where the major Endorphin releasing mechanisms lie. When Dopamine function declines, Endorphin function also declines. Hence, when too much stress causes failure of Dopamine function, it also causes loss of your body's natural "pain killer".

Dopamine also runs your body's "Pleasure Center". This is the area of your brain that allows you to enjoy life. When stress interferes with your Dopamine function, the Pleasure Center becomes inoperative. Normally pleasureful activities no longer give any pleasure. With severe Dopamine/Endorphin malfunction, life becomes painful and devoid of any pleasure.

When Dopamine runs low ....

life is NO LONGER enjoyable.

WHAT OVERSTRESS FEELS LIKE

When your stress level is high enough to cause failure of your Happy Messengers, what is going to happen to you? What will you feel like?

If your total stress load is high enough to interfere with your brain's Happy Messengers, then your Body Clock is going to stop working. You will find yourself having difficulty falling asleep, and frequent awakenings during the night, perhaps with vivid dreams. When morning rolls around, you will not feel at all rested (Serotonin malfunction).

Next, you will note lack of energy, lack of desire to get out and do things, lack of interest in the outside world (Noradrenalin malfunction).

Next, you will have aches and pains. Particularly common are chest, shoulder, back and neck pains. But, it will seem like you are aware of vague, uncomfortable feelings from all over our body. Along with increased sensitivity to aches and pains, there is a decreased sense of pleasure in life. Things that used to be fun or pleasurable do not seem enjoyable anymore (Dopamine/Endorphin malfunction).

When all of these symptoms coincide— lack of sleep, fatigue, aches and pains— you feel that life is not enjoyable anymore. You feel overwhelmed by life. Now you may cry easily, and feel that you are "depressed".

You may also feel quite anxious. All these strange changes in your body. Why can't I sleep? Why do I ache all the time? Am I having a heart attack? What is happening to me? It is not uncommon for persons who are experiencing the strange changes in their body caused by Happy Messenger failure to have periods of panic. It is during these so-called "panic attacks" that you feel as if you can not catch your breath. The heart races in panic, the muscles ache and pain all over the chest. You may even get light-headed. Stress has caused your body to behave in strange and difficult ways. Under these circumstances, anxiety and fear are not at all unexpected.

All of us have experienced some periods of OVERSTRESS in our lives. Usually they will be of short duration. We live in such a high stress society, however, that at least TEN PERCENT OF OUR POPULATION IS IN OVERSTRESS ALL THE TIME! These people, who have inherited a Low Stress Tolerance, are fighting against Happy Messenger failure every day of their lives. It rarely stops; and they are sorely afflicted.

In the past, we did not know the cause of this suffering. Such persons were often said to have a "mental illness". The medical world now recognizes these symptoms to arise from a brain Happy Messenger malfunction. THIS MALFUNCTION IS CAUSED BY TOO MUCH STRESS.

What was once regarded as a mental illness has emerged from that shadowy realm to reside in the world of biochemistry and physical illness.

5

Pick-Me-Up's

PICK ME UP'S

When you don't feel well, you normally try to do something to make yourself feel better. It turns out that all around you are substances which can temporarily make you feel better. Nature has provided a host of these Pick-Me-Up's that you can eat, drink, inhale or inject. All these Pick-Me-Up's work by chemically boosting one or more of your Happy Messenger levels, thus helping to temporarily restore balance to your OVERSTRESSED brain. A Pick-Me-Up can temporarily let you sleep better, help relieve an ache or pain, or give you energy. Here is a list of common Pick-Me-Up's that OVERSTRESSED people use. All of these work by virtue of causing an increase in Happy Messenger levels.

Sugar

The sugars: glucose (honey), lactose (milk sugar), fructose (fruit sugar), and sucrose (cane sugar) are called simple sugars. They are relatively tiny sugar molecules which are easily absorbed by the body. These sugars are absorbed so readily that placing honey under your tongue will cause an increase in blood sugar practically identical to injecting it intravenously. A sudden rise in blood sugar leads to an immediate boost in Happy Messenger levels. Simple sugars are, by far, the most popular and most widely used Pick-Me-Up.

Caffeine

Caffeine is a brain active drug that leaves your general blood circulation, enters your brain, and causes a boost in your brain Happy Messengers. We all are aware of caffeine's energizing capabilities, as caffeine is probably our second most widely used Pick-Me-Up. It is important to note that caffeine is found not only in coffee, but in chocolate, sodas, and many teas.

Alcohol

Drinking alcohol is a powerful booster of brain Happy Messengers. By boosting Serotonin function it helps the Body Clock function, which helps people sleep. By boosting Noradrenalin it helps people feel energized and aggressive. By boosting Endorphin it diminishes pain sensation and increases pleasure. Thus, it should not be surprising that the alcoholic may take a drink to fall asleep, take an "eye opener" to get going in the morning, have a drink to feel more in control when he goes in to see the boss, take a drink so he is "feeling no pain," or drink to make social gatherings "more fun." Alcohol is the third most widely used Pick-Me-Up.

Interestingly, solvents of various kinds can act as a Pick-Me-Up, having an effect similar to alcohol. The solvent vapors, when inhaled, enter the blood and act directly on the brain. There, they cause a boost in brain messenger levels and act as a Pick-Me-Up. Many solvents will do this: glues, cleaning fluids, nail polish remover, oil based paints. We mention these because most people who work around these solvents will not even realize that these solvents are directly affecting their brain, and acting as Pick-Me-Up's.

Tobacco, Marijuana, Cocaine, Amphetamines, Heroin

Tobacco, marijuana, cocaine, amphetamines, and heroin are chemicals that directly boost brain Happy Messenger function. They are widely used and extremely potent.

Your Own Adrenalin

As we mentioned earlier, when the body prepares to either fight, or run, a hormone called Adrenalin is released from the adrenal glands. Adrenalin is a cousin of Noradrenalin. Adrenalin release instantly boosts brain Noradrenalin function.

Remember how you almost fell asleep while driving? You caught yourself just before you crossed over the center divider to hit an oncoming car. Boy, did your heart beat, and you were certainly awake after that!

Many people use their own Adrenalin release as the Pick-Me-Up they need to feel healthy. A common instance of this is a "workaholic". The workaholic is terribly OVER-STRESSED. Instead of trying to reduce his stress load, however, his solution is to work sixteen to twenty hours a day, thus keeping himself "high" on his body's own Adrenalin release. Another example is to found among the persons who engage in high risk, "high excitement" sports or gambling. Here will be found many who are suffering from OVER-STRESS, and who use the sport or the gambling as their major Pick-Me-Up. Instead of reducing their stress level, these persons use their own Adrenalin to boost their brain Happy Messenger levels back toward normal.

HOW MANY OF THESE PICK-ME-UP'S DO _YOU_ USE EVERYDAY?

Sugar

☐ Milk   (LACTOSE)
☐ Fruit   (FRUCTOSE)
☐ Honey   (GLUCOSE)
☐ Cane or
      Beet Sugar   (SUCROSE)
☐ Corn Sweeteners   (FRUCTOSE)

(Eating whole fruit is OK. Fruit is beneficial for fiber and vitamins. But watch out for fruit juices and high fructose corn sweeteners, both of which are POTENT Pick-Me-Up's.)

Caffeine

☐ Coffee
☐ Black Tea
☐ Chocolate
☐ Colas

Alcohol

☐ Beer
☐ Wine
☐ Whiskey
☐ Liquor

Other Solvents

- ☐ Nail Polish Remover
- ☐ Paint Thinner
- ☐ Oil Based Paints
- ☐ Glues
- ☐ Gasoline Fumes

Your Own Adrenalin

- ☐ Workaholic
- ☐ Shopping Sprees
- ☐ Gambling Sprees
- ☐ Thrill Seeking Hobbies

Drugs

- ☐ Marijuana
- ☐ Cocaine
- ☐ Amphetamine
- ☐ Heroin

Tobacco

- ☐ Cigarettes
- ☐ Chewing Tobacco
- ☐ Snuff

Note how often they are all combined in the same product, i.e., a chocolate bar (sugar and caffeine); a chocolate rum cake (sugar, caffeine and alcohol); Kahlua with coffee and cream (sugar, caffeine, and alcohol). And often these are combined with a cigarette.

USING PICK-ME-UP'S IN STYLE

Persons who are in OVERSTRESS situations commonly use Pick-Me-Up's in two styles, "Maintenance" and "Binging".

Maintenance User

The Maintenance User tries to maintain a constant supply of Pick-Me-Up's at all times. John, for example, may have coffee in the morning to "wake up". Then he will have colas, coffee with milk, and assorted sweets during the day. An alcoholic beverage after dinner helps relaxation. And a drink at bedtime helps him fall asleep. Maybe the next day it will be three glasses of milk and eight chocolate chip cookies in the morning. The specific Pick-Me-Up used may vary each day, but John is always munching on some Pick-Me-Up. John is walking a tight rope, balancing his host of stressors on the one hand against this variety of "medicines" on the other. Pick-Me-Up's give him energy, Pick-Me-Up's help him relax, Pick-Me-Up's help him sleep.

Binging

Mary, on the other hand, may not use Pick-Me-Up's for weeks. But then, one day, she eats a whole box of chocolates, or three boxes of donuts, or two six packs of beer, or all of these things combined. Then, after this orgy of sugar, caffeine and/or alcohol, she is fine again for a long time.

The physiology behind John's behavior is clear. His stressors cause him to feel very uncomfortable. His Pick-Me-Up's help him to feel normal. So he uses Pick-Me-Up's as "medicines," medicines provided by nature, medicines that help him feel well.

But what about Mary? What could account for such a strange behavior on Mary's part? Why does she do without for long periods of time and then binge?

The answer lies in the depth of the brain, in a collection of brain cells known as ..."the Pleasure Center".

In the 1950's scientists began studying the effects of passing a minute electric current through certain parts of an animal's brain. In 1954 it was discovered that direct stimulation of certain brain areas could be extremely rewarding to an animal. Electrodes were implanted in the brain of a rat, and connected to a self-stimulation lever. (This is a lever inside the cage which the animal can press, sending a little electric current into its own brain.) To the amazement of the scientific community, self-stimulation of certain areas of the brain seemed so rewarding that an animal would endure severe punishment just to reach the lever and press it.

In 1965, one special area of the brain was discovered. Stimulation here was so rewarding that hungry rats, given a choice between eating, or pressing the lever, would choose to press the lever until they actually starved to death. By the late 1960's, the evidence was piling up. There appeared to be a group of areas in the brain that could give an intense reward to an animal whenever those areas were stimulated. These areas may be regarded collectively as... the Pleasure Center.

That such a Pleasure Center does exist in humans has been verified in neurosurgical operations. You see, the brain itself is devoid of pain fibers. So neurosurgery can be performed with the patient awake and alert. During certain surgeries, required by conditions such as tumors or severe epilepsy, the Pleasure Center of human beings has actually been stimulated. When the patient is basically comfortable and relaxed, the stimulation is reported as mildly pleasureful. But when the patient is depressed (when his Happy Messengers run low) the stimulation is reported as "wildly pleasureful". Indeed, such patients, given a button to press may stimulate themselves more than 400 times an hour.

This discovery is of great significance in the understanding of how Pick-Me-Up's work. It turns out that Pick-Me-Up's are capable of directly stimulating this very same Pleasure Center. By nature's design, the Pleasure Center relies on brain Happy Messengers for its stimulation. Hence, using Pick-Me-Up's boosts Happy Messenger levels, and directly stimulates the Pleasure Center.

If a person already has an adequate supply of Happy Messengers, the additional stimulation is nice, but not really compelling. But if OVERSTRESS has caused a large deficiency in Happy Messenger functioning (if one's Pleasure Center is, in effect, "starved" for Happy Messages) then the effect of the Pick-Me-Up is enormous. Just as the lever and electrode had led to an uncontrollable self-stimulation in the animal; just as the button and electrode had led to wild self-stimulation in the neurosurgical patient; so a Pick-Me-Up may lead to fits of uncontrollable — totally uncontrollable — self-stimulation in the Pick-Me-Up user. In the extreme case, such episodes of self-stimulation, such binges, may continue until the person is forced to vomit up his Pick-Me-Up's, or in the case of alcohol, until the person drinks himself to unconsciousness.

This explains why one person may take a Pick-Me-Up, an alcoholic beverage, for example, and find it mildly pleasureful, while someone with OVERSTRESS may take one drink and develop a bout of absolutely uncontrollable binging.

Cue Reactions

An important feature of Pick-Me-Up use is the so-called, "Cue Reaction". If you talk to binge chocolate eaters, or binge drinkers, or binge cookie eaters, they will often tell you that they really had no desire to have anything at all. They were just passing by the kitchen and noticed a bag of cookies that their roommate had bought for the picnic tomorrow. The next thing they knew, half the cookies were gone.

The smell of cookies baking, going over to mother's house, or even seeing a cookie advertisement in a magazine, can trigger cookie eating. In this case the trigger for eating was the mere sight of the cookies. In essence, a Cue Reaction is a type of conditioned reaction. Every time you are in a situation in which you take a Pick-Me-Up, be it a cookie or an alcoholic beverage, you forge a link in your brain between the situation and the Pick-Me-Up. Then, when you are in a similar situation, your body will automatically reach for the Pick-Me-Up. The beer industry has spent billions of dollars associating beer and professional sports. Can you imagine sports on television without beer advertisements?

When football comes on the air, the beer commercials cause Cue Reactions all over the country. Viewers head towards the refrigerator for a can of beer. These reactions are automatic. Usually the person is unaware of any association between the Cue and the Reaction. You are watching television, talking and joking, and suddenly there is a beer in your hand.

You see, the actual decision to drink the beer has been made at a deep and primitive area of the brain. Thinking occurs in our outer brain layers known as the CORTEX. But the inner SUB-CORTICAL layer is responsible for coordinating AUTOMATIC functions of the body. When you walk, your sub-cortical brain swings your arms to balance you, it adjusts the blood flow to your muscles, it regulates your body's temperature, and breathing. All of this is automatic. You never have to think about it.

Pavlov demonstrated how easily one may condition the sub-cortical brain. He trained dogs to salivate at the sound of a bell. The sound of a bell was not food, but he trained the dogs to salivate at the sound. Likewise, the beer companies have trained much of the public to grab a beer when they hear the sound of football. Football has nothing to do with beer, but people have been trained to associate the two. And the association occurs at a deep level, distinct from our consciousness. Turn on the TV, out comes the beer. No thinking involved, it's all automatic. If it were not effective, the beer companies would not spend billions each year on such viewer training.

The Maintenance Pick-Me-Up user will develop a set of very strong Cue Reactions. For instance, after breakfast must be coffee. The first work break, more coffee. Lunch includes a soft drink. Arrive home to take a glass of Chablis. Wine with dinner and another glass before bed. Because the conditioned use of Pick-Me-Up's is ingrained at a sub-cortical level, it becomes just as automatic as breathing in or out, or swinging your arms while walking. The Maintenance Pick-Me-Up user is no more aware of his use of Pick-Me-Up's than you are of your breathing right now. In fact, Pick-Me-Up's are so much a part of our life, and they are so automatic, that the Maintenance Pick-Me-Up'er is totally unaware that consumption of large amounts of simple sugar, caffeine, and alcohol are not "normal" or healthy for the body.

The Binge Pick-Me-Up user, on the other hand, may not use Pick-Me-Up's at all for long periods. But when OVERSTRESS conditions cause severe messenger imbalance in the brain, the stage is set for the binge. There, on the table, is a bag of cookies. Or here are the guys to watch the big football game. Boom, you have a binge. It is quick and it is automatic.

DRAW BACKS OF USING PICK ME UP'S

The symptoms of Happy Messenger failure: sleeping problems, aches and pains, lack of energy, lack of enjoyment of life, crying, depression, and panic attacks are brought on by conditions of OVERSTRESS. - - - TEN PERCENT OF OUR POPULATION IS FUNCTIONING IN OVERSTRESS RIGHT NOW- - - Many persons in our society feel "out of balance" quite regularly. The common Pick-Me-Up's, simple sugars, caffeine, alcohol, and tobacco are available all around us. In the United States at least twenty million people use them regularly to try and get themselves to feel "normal" again; to sleep well, to have enough energy, enjoy life, stop the anxiety or depression. Unfortunately, Pick-Me-Up's do not work very well.

The major drawback of the Pick-Me-Up's is the fact that: YOU CAN NEVER ACCURATELY REBALANCE YOUR BRAIN MESSENGERS USING PICK-ME-UP'S. That is something only your own body can do. It is just too delicate a chemical adjustment. Try as you will, you will never be able to make yourself feel right using Pick-Me-Up's. DESPITE THE USE OF PICK-ME-UP'S, A PERSON WHO IS SUFFERING FROM OVERSTRESS WILL CONTINUE TO FEEL "UNBALANCED".

By using Pick-Me-Up's, the person merely puts himself into a shaky equilibrium where he tries to balance a host of stressors, on the one hand, against a variety of Pick-Me-Up's on the other. Since it is impossible for a person to accurately rebalance his brain chemistry this way, he will sometimes feel "OK," but much of the time will have the mood swings, poor sleep and depression of Happy Messenger failure. His will be a constant up-and-down roller coaster of feeling well and feeling ill.

When you rely on Pick-Me-Up's....

You ride a ROLLER COASTER of emotions.

6

Stress Tolerance: Patterns of Inheritance

STRESS TOLERANCE: PATTERNS OF INHERITANCE

Most people can handle the stresses of modern life, stresses considered "normal" in our society, without developing any problems. But about ten percent of our population cannot handle these stresses. ONE IN TEN PERSONS IS FUNCTIONING IN OVERSTRESS RIGHT NOW—AT STRESS LEVELS THE OTHER NINE HANDLE WITHOUT ANY PROBLEM. The reason these people are more susceptible to stress is that they have inherited a Low Stress Tolerance. These persons develop Happy Messenger failure at levels of stress that others handle with ease. For a person with this inherited problem, 150 on the stress scale is enough to affect Happy Messenger function, and cause OVERSTRESS. For most people, OVERSTRESS may be a temporary condition, but for these ten percent of persons, OVERSTRESS is a life-long problem. In our society, if you can not handle a 150 stress level, you will be in OVERSTRESS forever.

Such persons typically show signs of OVERSTRESS when they approach their teen years. As we have seen, the teen years are one of the most stressful times of a person's life. When a child who inherits a Low Stress Tolerance enters the teen years, fatigue, sleep problems, depression, crying spells, and anxiety may become manifest.

The teenager will begin to rely on Pick-Me-Up's as "medicines" to make him or her feel better. Patterns of binging or maintenance with Pick-Me-Up's will be established. And the person will often be stuck for the rest of his or her life on the wild roller coaster:

...A host of stressors on the one hand, balanced by

67

alcohol, sugar, caffeine, and an army of Pick-Me-Up's on the other. It is a constant juggling act which serves to partially normalize brain function for a few hours, followed by a crash, and then more Pick-Me-Up "medicine"...

This Low Stress Tolerance is an inherited characteristic, and runs very strongly in families. If you keep in mind the broad range of Pick-Me-Up's that people use, it is very easy to spot families where Pick-Me-Up use is rampant. Since the inherited problem is Low Stress Tolerance, you will see numerous family members with signs of OVERSTRESS: sleep problems, fatigue, depression, anxiety, all occurring at stress levels that appear "normal" in our society. Most of the members of the family will have learned to "treat" themselves with some type of Pick-Me-Up. They will use their Pick-Me-Up in either a binge or maintenance style.

Thus, the person you are talking to may be complaining of fatigue, crying, being overwhelmed by life, or anxiety attacks. One or both parents may have been an alcoholic (more often the parent of the same sex), a brother may be a workaholic. Someone else in the family may have stopped drinking alcohol but smokes three packs per day, eats ice cream, sweets, and coffee all day long. The variations are endless, but the findings are the same. Pick-Me-Up use is rampant in many families, practically non-existent in others.

But, you may ask, how do we know that this is an inherited problem? How do we know that the extensive use of Pick-Me-Up's in the family is not caused by the family environment? Wouldn't it be plausible that an alcoholic father would have an alcoholic son because the son would have "learned to drink alcohol"? Wouldn't it be plausible that families that use Pick-Me-Up's teach their children to use Pick-Me-Up's also?

A very interesting study has been done looking at children who were given up for adoption at birth. Thousands of children were involved. These children were placed in new homes right after they were born. They never knew their biological parents. The topic of the study was the pattern of the use of the Pick-Me-Up, alcohol.

The study produced several surprising findings. The first was that children who did not have an alcoholic <u>biologic</u> parent were not likely to become alcoholics, even if they were raised by alcoholic foster parents. Thus, merely being raised by an alcoholic in no way caused children to become alcoholics.

On the other hand, sons whose <u>biologic</u> fathers were alcoholics, were nine times more likely to be alcoholics. And daughters whose <u>biologic</u> mothers were alcoholics were three times more likely to become alcoholics -- even though the children knew nothing about their biologic parents!

This study on adopted children has been interpreted to show that alcoholism is an inherited disease. What it actually shows, however, is that Low Stress Tolerance is an inherited condition. "Alcoholism" is not the disease, it is merely the major Pick-Me-Up that the person is using to try to "medicate" himself.

In previous years, it was not recognized that the various Pick-Me-Up's work in a similar fashion. These Pick-Me-Up's serve as "medicines" that a person uses to try and make himself/herself feel more normal again. All the Pick-Me-Up's work by temporarily boosting the function of Happy Messengers.

Since this common mechanism of action is still not widely recognized, it is common to hear people speak of the use of a specific Pick-Me-Up as a "disease" in-and-of itself.

For instance people talk about "alcoholics," and the disease of "alcoholism". They speak of "work-a-holics," "compulsive gamblers," "compulsive eaters," and "cocaine addicts," as if the use of each specific Pick-Me-Up was a separate disease.

In reality, most of these persons have the same under-lying problem: an OVERSTRESS which makes them feel ill, and for which they are attempting to treat themselves with some form of Pick-Me-Up. These persons are merely trying to cope, as best they can, with OVERSTRESS.

(This landmark study can be found in the literature under: Bohman, "Inheritance of Alcoholism: cross fostering analy-sis of adopted men", Arch of Gen Psychiatry 1981, vol. 38 pp. 861-868; See also same volume pp. 965-969 for cross fostering analysis of adopted women.)

7

Pick-Me-Up
Rebound

PICK-ME-UP REBOUND

We mentioned that you can never accurately rebalance your brain chemistry with Pick-Me-Up's. We now know that at least one in ten of us, those who inherit Low Stress Tolerance, spend much of their life trying to do just that.

There are three reasons you cannot restore brain chemistry to normal using Pick-Me-Up's. One, as we have mentioned, is that the minute changes in chemical levels, are beyond your ability to adjust "by hand". It is like trying to level the earth in a small flower pot, when the only tool you have is a four ton bulldozer. You are going to end up with a cracked pot.

The second is the fact that all Pick-Me-Up's cause rebound. That is, they quickly make you feel well. But when the Pick-Me-Up wears off, you will feel sick just as quickly. For example, if you eat three donuts and drink coffee with cream and sugar, you are giving yourself a big slug of sugar and caffeine. This causes a quick boost in Happy Messenger levels, resulting in a rapid upswing toward normal levels of energy, a normal pain threshold, and an improved sense of well-being. But as fast as this boost is, that is how fast the subsequent fall will be -- toward lack of energy, fatigue, aches and pains and feeling ill. The quicker and more effective the boost, the quicker and steeper the fall. This phenomenon is called Pick-Me-Up Rebound.

People who have inherited a Low Stress Tolerance, who rely on Pick-Me-Up's to try and feel normal, end up suffering from wild mood swings. Some days they are pleasant, happy and energetic. Other days they are moody, depressed, or anxious.

What they should be doing, of course, is trying to

LOWER THEIR STRESS LEVELS !! If one can lower one's stress level enough to be out of OVERSTRESS, the body will rebalance itself.

But, most people in OVERSTRESS never think of reducing their stress levels. They don't even realize they are suffering from too much stress. They have been in OVER-STRESS for so many years that they think this is what ev-eryone feels like. So they do the best they can, medicating themselves with Pick-Me-Up's, and wondering why they "feel lousy" most of the time. They go to doctors who tell them that there is "nothing wrong," or that they are "depressed," or having "anxiety attacks", or that they are "alcoholic".

It is a very frustrating experience for these people. So, they continue to use coffee, sugar, alcohol and other Pick-Me-Up's to try and feel normal again. But in doing so, they just make the roller coaster ride steeper, faster, and wilder.

ADAPTATION

The third problem with Pick-Me-Up's is that the body quickly adapts to many of them. This means that a person has to take ever increasing amounts of Pick-Me-Up to achieve the desired effect. A person may begin by using one cup of coffee a day, and end up drinking a potful; or smoking five cigarettes a day, and end up smoking two packs; or drinking two drinks a day, and end up with a pint.

People use these Pick-Me-Up's as medicines, trying to boost brain Happy Messenger function. But like any medi-cine, Pick-Me-Up's have side effects. When the body adapts, and the person has to use large quantities of his/her "medi-cine", the side effects of the caffeine, alcohol, tobacco, and drugs become very serious.

A person using large amounts of alcohol is at high risk

74

of hurting others, or of dying from a traffic accident, liver failure, or bleeding complications. Heavy tobacco use damages the lungs and arteries and causes cancer. Lots of caffeine can cause abnormal heart rhythms. Heavy doses of the illegal drugs can easily lead to convulsions, overdose, or death. All of these side effects add more stress to the body, which just worsens the OVERSTRESS.

For all these reasons; the inability to balance your brain chemistry "by hand"; the rebound crash caused by the Pick-Me-Up's; and the severe side effects of heavy doses; using Pick-Me-Up's _prevents_ stability. Using Pick-Me-Up's as medicine leads to the rollercoaster of ill health.

DANGEROUS TEEN-AGE YEARS

Now let us review what happens to at least one in ten persons. They inherit a Low Stress Tolerance. They go into OVERSTRESS usually in the teenage years. They become depressed, withdrawn, do not seem to enjoy life, complain of aches and pains. People around them tell the parents, "don't worry, teenagers are always like this".

The person begins to use Pick-Me-Up's. He or she is seen to be sometimes bright, cheerful and energetic, sometimes moody, depressed and withdrawn. Pick-Me-Up use begins to settle into a style of Maintenance or Binging. Either way, the roller coaster ride becomes steeper and faster. Finally, the person reaches a shaky equilibrium between the host of stressors, on the one hand, and his or her "medicines" on the other hand.

Although the Pick-Me-Up's help the person "feel more normal" in the short run, they hurt the person in the long run. All of the Pick-Me-Up's make the person feel worse than they were to begin with. As long as the person relies on the Pick-Me-Up to try and feel normal, instead of reducing total stress load, he/she is condemned to the emotional roller coaster. Sometimes well, but sometimes irritable, fatigued, anxious or depressed, the teenager just cannot seem to level out his/her emotions. If this pattern is not interrupted in the teenage years, by helping the teenager deal properly with OVERSTRESS, he/she is quite likely to be facing a life-long losing struggle.

"IT HURTS SO GOOD"

The attribute of helping in the short run, yet doing harm in the long run is what we refer to as "hurting so good". This is perfectly exemplified in one of society's most commonly used substances, cigarettes. People use cigarettes as a Pick-Me-Up, helping to boost their sagging Happy Messengers. At the same time, the cigarettes cause severe long term damage to your body. This increases the stress that caused the need for cigarettes in the first place. This vicious cycle, which "hurts so good", is characteristic of all the most addicting substances found in our society.

As an instructive exercise, let us try and design the perfect addicting substance for human beings. Let us call it "Addict-o-matic".

First of all, we have seen that all the Pick-Me-Up's cause rebound. The sugar high, for example, will be followed by the sugar low. Although sugar may temporarily make the person feel better, the deep rebound will make him feel worse again, so he will want more Pick-Me-Up. That sounds like a good place to begin our designing. Let us throw a nice concentrated lump of simple sugar into our potion.

We can do even better if we put in a few more Pick-Me-Up's. For these Pick-Me-Up's let us select ones that lead to adaptation. Yes, let us add some caffeine next. Caffeine produces a nice rebound low. In addition, the body will adapt to the presence of the caffeine. At first, one cup of Addict-o-matic will give a person quite a brain messenger jolt, but as time goes on, the body becomes used to the presence of the caffeine. Now it may take three cups, a pot, or three pots of Addict-o-matic to produce the same effect. As the person gets used to the caffeine, his Addict-o-matic consumption must go up for the Pick-Me-Up's to work. Then, his sugar consumption will skyrocket. This will cause wonderful new peaks and valleys in his blood sugar and really make the roller coaster ride wild. Yes, sugar and caffeine together make a pretty good Addict-o-matic. (Do you know anyone that drinks coffee with sugar by the potful every day?)

But wait a minute, there is another Pick-Me-Up that people become tolerant to: alcohol. Let us throw in an ounce of whiskey. As the person develops a tolerance to the effects of alcohol, it will take ever increasing amounts of alcohol to achieve the same brain messenger boost. This means larger amounts of Addict-o-matic, and even wilder ups and downs of the personal roller coaster.

At this point we surely must have designed the most wicked addictor, don't you think?

Actually, we can do even worse. What do you think would happen if we could, somehow, slip something into the potion -- something that would intensify the person's STRESS LOAD?

If our potion could increase the person's stress load, it would make his OVERSTRESS worse, which would increase his need for Pick-Me-Up's. The beauty of this scheme is that the same potion that supplies the Pick-Me-Up's would then also supply more stress. This, in turn, would make the person need more Pick-Me-Up. It is a vicious cycle.

We can increase the person's stress load with Addict-o-matic if we add some small amount of poison to it. The poison acts as a stressor, increasing the need for Pick-Me-Up's. But the poison has to be mild. If it is too strong, the person will get too sick, and he won't drink the Addict-o-matic. Well, it turns out that we already have the poison in the Addict-o-matic. Alcohol is a liver poison, directly killing or damaging liver cells. This damage will add more stress to the body, making the Addict-o-matic much more potent.

(It is interesting to note that alcohol plays two separate roles in Addict-o-matic. First, it has a Pick-Me-Up effect, immediately boosting brain Happy Messenger levels. Then, it has a slower role as a poison, causing a worsening of the OVERSTRESS).

We can also increase the person's stress load by adding certain allergy-causing food substances to the Addict-o-matic. We know that the most common food sensitivities are to milk, corn and yeast. Since we are leaving no stone unturned, let us dump all of these foods into Addict-o-matic. Let's use a high fructose corn sweetener for our simple sugar, add that right to the caffeine and alcohol, and then put in some milk.

We don't have to worry about the yeast, because it was added to the mix when we added the alcohol. You see, alcohol is produced by yeast fermentation of sugar. Every alcoholic beverage <u>already</u> contains bits of yeast protein. So when we added alcohol, we also added bits of yeast.

OK, now we have concocted the perfect Addict-o-matic. It contains one, or all, of the common Pick-Me-Up's: Simple sugar, caffeine, and alcohol. It also contains one, or all, of the common food allergens: milk, corn, and yeast. In addition, the most potent version of Addict-o-matic contains a mild poison, such as alcohol. Of course, it is even better if you smoke a cigarette with it!

In reality, you can construct Addict-o-matic, or buy it ready made at any grocery or liquor store. Without the alcohol, you can get it at a restaurant, movie theater or ball game. It's called rum and cola, Kahlua and cream, Mexican coffee, beer, rum cake, chocolate bar, wine, etc. Most of our "junk food snacks" are simple or complicated versions of Addict-o-matic. That is why they are in such high demand; that is why they are sold everywhere.

8

Put-Me-Down's

PUT ME DOWN'S

Consider John, a person struggling with OVER-STRESS. He can't get a restful sleep, has aches and pains, and anxiety attacks. "What is wrong with me?" he moans, "I'm having chest, neck and back pain. I feel lousy. I can't go on this way. Life is not enjoyable anymore...." John works fourteen hours a day, drinks coffee and takes sweets all day long. He has a few drinks in the evening to "relax". But his Pick-Me-Up's only make his roller coaster ride steeper and bumpier. Sometimes he feels "OK", but much of the time he is a "mass of jangled nerves".

So, in exasperation, he goes to the doctor. "Can't you give me something to calm down my nerves and let me get a good night's sleep?" John says. "I just can't handle this anymore."

The doctor, in all likelihood, will respond by giving John a prescription for a PUT-ME-DOWN. Put-Me-Down's are medicines that temporarily force the body into sleeping or tranquilizing.

The most well known of these drugs is Valium. (Valium has quite a few relatives that work the same way but are known by different names: Tranxene, Serax, Xanax, Ativan, Centrax, Paxipam, and Librium are some examples.) Chemically, all the drugs in the Valium family are known as benzodiazepines. Another family of Put-Me-Down's are the barbiturates. These are such medicines as Phenobarbitol, Butalbitol, and Seconal.

The Put-Me-Down's do not work via the brain's Happy Messengers. Instead, they affect the brain at their own unique receptor sites. Unfortunately, Put-Me-Down's only work for one to three months. After that, the receptors adapt to the presence of the Put-Me-Down's. Then the person's aches, pains and fatigue come right back again. Unfortunately, by that time, many people find it impossible to stop the Put-Me-Down.

Benzodiazepines (the Valium family) are notorious for this. They have such a severe withdrawal syndrome that people taking them for any extended period of time cannot get off them - - even though the Put-Me-Down is no longer doing any good!

We know that a person cannot chemically balance his brain with Pick-Me-Up's. They just make the roller coaster ride worse. Add Put-Me-Down's to the potpourri of chemicals, and it becomes that much more hopeless. Can you imagine how futile an effort it is to balance microscopic amounts of chemicals in your brain with sugar, caffeine, alcohol and a Put-Me-Down too?!? Unfortunately, it is impossible for a person to feel anywhere near normal for any stable length of time.

Yet, so many people go to the doctor trying to find a way to feel rested, or to calm their raw OVERSTRESSED nerves, that benzodiazepines like Valium are the most commonly prescribed brain active medicines in the country today. (Remember, one in every ten of us is OVERSTRESSED right now.)

How to Deal with OVERSTRESS

Depression, anxiety attacks, hypochondriasis, alcoholism, compulsive gambling, insomnia, stress-o-holism, these are all names given to SYMPTOMS of OVERSTRESS; or to the major Pick-Me-Up that the person is using for self-medication. In the past, each of these has been thought to be a disease in-and-of itself. We now know that each of these is not a disease in-and-of itself but may be a result of Happy Messenger malfunction, and the person's largely futile efforts to self-medicate with Pick-Me-Up's or Put-Me-Down's. The great breakthrough of the 1980's has been our understanding of how all this works. We now have tools that can help a person suffering from OVERSTRESS to feel healthy again, sleep well, and be rid of aches, pains, anxiety, and depression.

9

The
Treatment of
OVERSTRESS

★★★★★★★★★★★★★★★★★★★

The BIGGEST MISTAKE you
can make in handling stress is...

Using Pick-Me-Up's to boost
your Happy Messengers, while
continuing to pile on the stress.

When you do this, you
"Ride the Wild Rollercoaster":
Sometimes feeling well,
mostly feeling ill,
never acheiving balance.

★★★★★★★★★★★★★★★★★★★

★★★★★★★★★★★★★★★★★★★

What you should do is...

Stop using the Pick-Me-Up's,
lower your stress level,
and give your body a chance
to re-balance itself.

Then you can acheive
balance, feel well,
and STAY well.

★★★★★★★★★★★★★★★★★★★

OVERSTRESS IS TREATED
by
REDUCING YOUR STRESS LOAD

Add up your Stress Scale points for the past twelve months. If it is above 250, you should be keenly alert for the early signs of OVERSTRESS.   Even a level of 150 will OVERSTRESS ten percent of persons. For this reason, it is best to aim for a continuing stress load of below 150 on the Stress Scale.

Here are
TEN SIMPLE WAYS
to
REDUCE YOUR STRESS LOAD. . . .

1.

MAKE YOUR LIFE REGULAR...
as "clock work"

If you suffer from OVERSTRESS, you have disrupted the function of your Body Clock. Re-setting your Body Clock is vital if you are to feel well, sleep soundly, and awake refreshed. Give yourself a definite wake up and sleep time. This sets a frame of reference for your Body Clock. It will take two to three weeks to synchronize your Body Clock to your schedule. So, stick to your schedule!!

But what if I try to go to sleep at 10 p.m. and I can't fall asleep? Or what if I fall asleep but keep waking up during the night?

Sleep difficulty is the hallmark of OVERSTRESS. When your Body Clock stops working, you may have trouble falling asleep and staying asleep. Or, conversely, you may feel sleepy all the time. Either symptom may be produced when the Body Clock stops working. It all depends on which "position" the Clock was in when it stops: wakefulness, or sleepiness.

So, do not expect to have your sleep problems go away until your Body Clock is working again. Go ahead and set yourself a reasonable wake up time and bed time. Do the best you can to stick to these times. As you lower your stress levels, your Body Clock will begin to work. It will then match its cycle of wakefulness and sleep to the times that you have set for it. Remember, this process will take at least three weeks, so stick firmly to your time schedule.

But what if I put myself to bed at my bed time, and I just lie there without falling asleep?

If, after 45 minutes, you have not fallen asleep, get up and read a book or do something around the house. Sooner or later, you will feel sleepy and fall asleep. Keep putting yourself to bed at your bed time every night. As you reduce your stress levels, your Body Clock will begin working. Your Body Clock will gradually match your chosen sleep schedule. In the meantime, be patient and work to reduce your stress levels as much as possible.

If You Must Do "Shift Work":

Your Body Clock will always try and synchronize itself with your daily schedule. If your job requires you to work varying shifts, however, you may have difficulty in getting your Body Clock to match your shift. When properly synchronized, your Body Clock tells you to be awake for your work, and tells you to go to sleep after your work. If you do evening work, your Body Clock will shift itself so that you will be awake for your evening work, and be able to sleep during the day. But this change requires two or three weeks to occur. If your employer rotates your shift more often than every two or three weeks, your Body Clock will always be mismatched with your work requirements. You will be trying to work when your body wants to sleep, and trying to sleep when your body wants to work. This will make it practically impossible to restore the proper functioning of your Body Clock.

If you are OVERSTRESSED, you should avoid "shift work" if at all possible. If you MUST do "shift work", try and work at least three weeks at each shift before rotating to a new one. And always make sure the direction of shift rotation is "morning to evening to night to morning again". (Never try to rotate shifts in the reverse direction. Your Body Clock will blow a fuse.)

Trying to work when your body wants to sleep ....

Trying to sleep when your body wants to work ....

If Your Work Involves Air Travel to Different Time Zones:

Those of you who do frequent long-distance air traveling will be familiar with the condition known as "Jet Lag". Jet Lag occurs when you board an airplane and rapidly move to an area where the local time is more than three to four hours different than the time on your Body Clock. You might, for instance, board a jet in Hawaii and fly to New York. When you arrive in New York, it might be midnight New York Time, but only 6 p.m. on your Body Clock.

All your body rhythms: temperature, stress-fighting hormone, sleep cycles are now out of synchronization with your local time zone. Now you are trying to go to sleep when your body is still awake, and trying to work when your body expects you to be getting ready for bed. It will take two to three weeks for your Body Clock to harmonize with your new surroundings. During that time it is not unusual to be fatigued and to feel "not with it". We call this feeling "Jet Lag".

If you are OVERSTRESSED, you should avoid inter-time zone traveling. But if you MUST change time zones, try to wait at least three weeks between trips. And when you do take that trip, and you arrive in a new time zone, it will be easier for you to adjust if you stay up later, rather than trying to force yourself to sleep when your body wants to be awake.

Changing time zones can

confuse your Body Clock

If You Work Indoors:

Your Body Clock requires exposure to daylight during the day in order to remain synchronized with your local time zone. Normal fluorescent lighting does not have the same light spectrum as daylight, hence it will NOT help your Body Clock to properly set itself. If you are a person who arises when it is dark, works indoors all day, and goes home when it is dark, your Body Clock may become out of phase with the world around you – – giving you a case of permanent "Jet Lag".

Because of this problem, manufacturers of fluorescent lights have begun producing "daylight spectrum" fluorescent lights. These lights will allow your Body Clock to synchronize itself with your work schedule.

If you work indoors, try to work by a window. If you can not, then see if you can have "daylight spectrum" fluorescent light bulbs installed. It really helps.

As an alternative for people who never see the sun, one can sit facing 600 watts of daylight spectrum fluorescent lights, three feet in front of you, for one hour. Do this at the time that you wish your Body Clock to learn to wake you up. You may eat breakfast, read a book, or watch television, but the light must be facing you.

Note that persons living in northern climates lacking in sunshine may have the same problem of permanent "Jet Lag". For these people the above suggestions will be equally helpful.

2.

GIVE YOURSELF A BREAK TODAY

You must give your body adequate time to repair itself, and to regenerate Happy Messengers. If you are having symptoms of OVERSTRESS:

Fatigue
Aches and pains
Anxiety
Problems sleeping
Lack of enjoyment of life
Depression

Give your body a chance to heal itself.

Every morning make a list of things that you want to get done...

THEN, CUT OFF THE BOTTOM HALF OF THIS LIST!

3.

LIGHTEN UP YOUR LOAD OF SOCIAL ENGAGEMENTS

Let someone else do the holiday dinner for the family, or make it a pot-luck on paper plates.

Only go out once this week.

Tell your visitors from out of town (who always expect to stay at your house) to call you "just as soon as they get settled in a hotel room".

SAY "NO" A LOT MORE OFTEN TO REQUESTS FROM OTHERS FOR YOUR TIME.

4.

POSTPONE MAKING ANY CHANGES IN YOUR LIVING ENVIRONMENT

Remember, CHANGE IS STRESS. So relax, postpone any big moves or changes for awhile.

* Postpone remodeling your home or apartment.

* Postpone moving to a new house or apartment.

Making a change in your living environment, even if it is a change that you are excited about, is a major stress. It will add a minimum of 25 stress points to your life; and, if it is a financial strain, may add as much as 65 stress points!

When you consider that you would like to reduce your stress level to 150 or below, you will see why postponing a change in your living environment will be very helpful in obtaining that goal.

5.

REDUCE THE NUMBER OF HOURS YOU SPEND AT WORK OR SCHOOL

If you are a "work-a-holic", or a "school-a-holic", you need to reduce the energy drain you are placing on your body. Work or school more than 40 hours per week adds 40 stress points to your life.

TAKE SOME TIME OFF

6.

THE OVERSTRESS DIET

Keep Your Blood Sugar Steady

People who are OVERSTRESSED almost always begin to use sugar as a Pick-Me-Up. Their blood sugar goes up and down wildly. Thus, the most important dietary consideration is to keep your blood sugar from swinging high, or swinging low. In order to feel well, you must level out your blood sugar, avoiding the "sugar highs", and "sugar lows". Take your sugar in the form of complex carbohydrates, such as cereals, rice, pasta, bread and potatoes. These foods, comprised of tightly interlinked sugars, are broken down slowly by the body, releasing their sugar over a long period of time. Eating frequent small meals, instead of a few large ones, also helps keep your blood sugar stable.

Eat More Vegetables

Your brain's production of one of the Happy Messengers, Serotonin, is sensitive to your diet. Eating more vegetables, can increase your brain's Serotonin production. This increase is due to improved absorption of the amino acid L-Tryptophan. (Vegetables contain the natural, safe, form of L-Tryptophan. At the present writing, synthetic L-Tryptophan has been removed from health food stores due to probable impurities that were, in some cases, causing severe and even fatal illness).

Meats contain natural L-Tryptophan also, but when you eat meats the L-Tryptophan has to compete with so many other amino acids for absorption that the L-Tryptophan loses out. The net result is that you get better absorption of L-Tryptophan when you eat vegetables.

In other words -- eat a salad for lunch.

You should also take a good multi-vitamin and mineral preparation. Here is a formula which is representative of such a vitamin. Such a vitamin is available at most any drug store. It is best to take such a vitamin once each day.

Vitamin A	5000 I.U.
Vitamin E	30 I.U.
Vitamin C	90 mg
Folic Acid	400 mcg
Vitamin B1 (Thiamine)	2.25 mg
Vitamin B2 (Riboflavin)	2.6 mg
Niacinamide	20 mg
Vitamin B6 (Pyridoxine)	3 mg
Vitamin B12	9 mcg
Vitamin D	400 I.U.
Biotin	45 mcg
Pantothenic Acid	10 mg
Calcium	162 mg
Phosphorus	125 mg
Iodine	150 mcg
Iron	27 mg
Magnesium	100 mg
Copper	2 mg
Manganese	5 mg
Potassium	30 mg
Chloride	27.2 mg
Chromium	25 mcg
Molybdenum	25 mcg
Selenium	25 mcg
Zinc	15 mg
Vitamin K1	25 mcg

"GET RID OF THE SUGAR...
WE CAN'T TAKE ANY MORE
OF THESE UPS AND DOWNS!"

7.

REDUCE YOUR USE OF PICK-ME-UP'S

Beware of Cue Reactions

To cut down on your intake of Pick-Me-Up's, remove them from the house, and any other place that is within easy reach. Do not forget to clear out your desk drawer at work, and the glove compartment of the car. Even though you want to reduce your sugar, caffeine, tobacco or alcohol consumption, just the sight of a cookie can lead you to eat it; just the sight of a beer can lead you to drink it – – before you even have a chance to stop yourself.

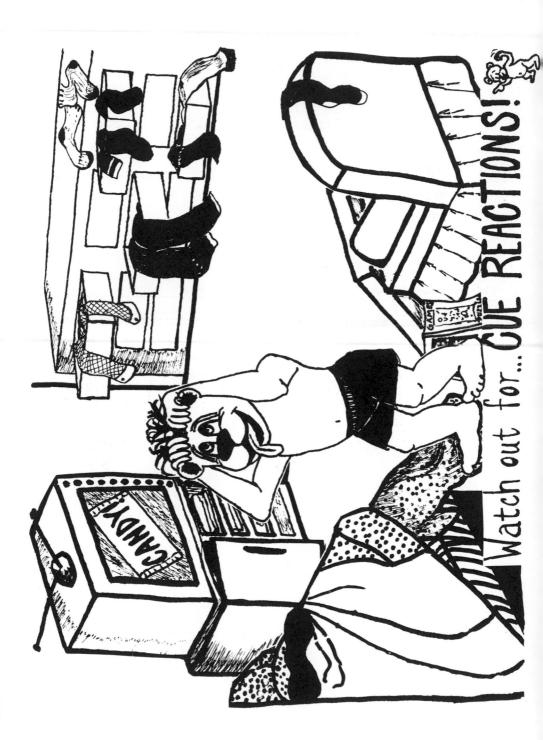

Watch out for... CUE REACTIONS!

8.

AVOID ALLERGIES

Allergy is a major source of stress for many of us. If there are certain things that trigger YOUR allergies, you should avoid them.

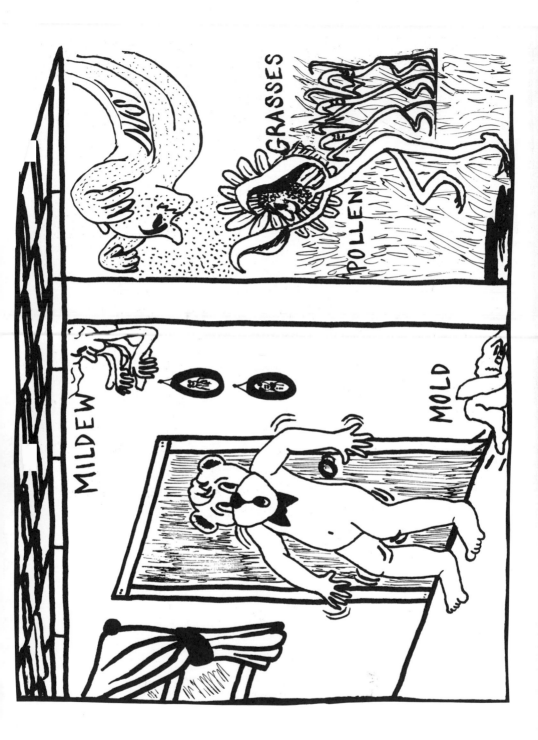

9.

START AN ENJOYABLE EXERCISE REST YOUR MIND

Begin an exercise that you enjoy. Preferably, do something that brings you into contact with other people. The value of such exercise, three times a week for 20 minutes to two hours, can not be over emphasized. Enjoyable exercise, in moderation, boosts your HAPPY MESSENGERS in a smooth sustained fashion. It will make you feel better right away!

Exercise has another beneficial effect. Most people, when exercising, do not worry. They are actually resting the nerve cells in the brain that worry, giving those cells time to renew their stores of HAPPY MESSENGERS, so they can function normally the next time they are needed.

There are other ways of "resting your mind". Dancing, listening to music, reading, working on a craft, playing a musical instrument, meditiation, self relaxation, and biofeedback also relieve stress. Any activity which concentrates your attention on a subject other than life's problems will help rest your mind. This rests the "Problem Solving" part of your brain, allowing it to regenerate HAPPY MESSENGERS and renew itself.

10.

STOP YOUR PUT-ME -DOWN'S

Tranquilizers and calmatives will prevent your body from restoring its Happy Messengers. Unlike Pick-Me-Up's, which can usually be taken in modest amounts without harm, Put-Me-Down's should be avoided altogether.

By reducing your stress load, stabilizing your blood sugar, improving your diet, avoiding allergies, and getting some exercise, you will find you will not want tranquilizers and calmatives. <u>Before stopping any prescription medicine, however, always check with your doctor</u>. We do not want you to accidentally stop a heart medicine or anti-epilepsy medication. Also, many of the Put-Me-Down's must be tapered down slowly, rather than stopped abruptly. Ask your doctor how fast you can stop your Put-Me-Down's.

(If someone has given you Put-Me-Down's to help you sleep, particularly the ones in the Valium family, you may have a real problem stopping them. They are best tapered off very slowly, and under medical supervision. Even then, the withdrawal symptoms from these drugs are very unpleasant. The chief withdrawal symptom is inability to sleep, and vivid disturbing dreams. If you try to stop them on your own, you may experience sleeplessness that is worse than ever! Then you may erroneously conclude that you need more, not less of the Put-Me-Down! It is very easy to be trapped by Put-Me-Down's.)

IF YOU ARE STILL NOT GETTING BETTER...

If you have done all of the preceding, and still have significant symptoms of OVERSTRESS:

Fatigue
Aches and pains
Anxiety
Problems sleeping
Lack of enjoyment of life
Depression

THEN IT IS TIME YOU OBTAINED SOME ASSISTANCE...

VISIT YOUR DOCTOR

OVERSTRESS that you can not clear up yourself may be the earliest warning sign of some hidden illness.

* Thyroid disease
* Calcium imbalance (too much or too little)
* Anemia
* Diabetes
* Manic-depression
* Liver disease
* Kidney malfunction
* Vitamin deficiency

These are examples of physical illnesses that you might not be aware of – – but which cause enough stress on your body to create OVERSTRESS.

Your doctor should do a complete physical examination, including tests on blood and urine. The automated blood testing machines can do a complete blood count, as well as measure your thyroid function, liver enzymes, kidney function, calcium and phosphorus, iron and blood sugar for a very reasonable price.

So, if your symptoms are not getting better with the TEN SIMPLE STEPS – – be sure to see your doctor.

ELIMINATE YOUR PICK-ME-UP'S ENTIRELY

If cutting down your Pick-Me-Up's did not get you off the "roller-coaster" of Pick-Me-Up high and Pick-Me-Up low, then you need to ELIMINATE Pick-Me-Up's entirely. You need to get off the "roller coaster" in order to start feeling well.

If you have a heavy intake of Pick-Me-Ups, do not despair. Today, physicians have many ways to help you stop your Pick-Me-Up's. A brain chemical re-balancer can support your Happy Messengers while you eliminate the Pick-Me-Ups from your system. Also, your doctor has other medications that can specifically block the craving for most Pick-Me-Up's. (Such a medicine is Clonidine.) These medicines must be prescribed by a physician after evaluating whether they are safe for you. If you are a heavy user of alcohol, sugar, caffeine, cigarettes, cocaine, heroin or ANY of the Pick-Me-Up's, effective medical treatment is now available to allow you to stop your Pick-Me-Up's, lower your stress level, re-balance your Happy Messengers, and enjoy life again.

ELIMINATE FOODS WHICH CAUSE BAD REACTIONS

If a certain food makes you wheeze, or gives you a stuffy nose, or diarrhea, or red itchy bumps on your skin, you should obviously avoid that food. Any allergic reaction of this type is a stress on your body which will contribute to your OVERSTRESS.

There is another type of food reaction you should avoid. ANY FOOD THAT YOU CRAVE OR BINGE is a brain active food. You are craving or binging it because it is directly affecting your brain. Most of the time these are foods which contain the Pick-Me-Up's, sugar or caffeine. But sometimes the substance in the food is corn, milk, or yeast protein. Many people have sensitivity reactions to corn, milk, or yeast containing products. The proteins in these substances directly affect brain messenger function. If, by this point in the book, you are STILL not feeling well, try a corn-free, milk-free, and/or a yeast-free diet. (Consult a dietician, or your doctor for a source of recipes).

VISIT A PROFESSIONAL COUNSELOR

An experienced counselor can be of great help! It is often possible for a counselor to pinpoint stressors which you may have overlooked. Counselors can help you handle general life problems in ways that produce less stress. You should specifically seek instruction in self-relaxation, biofeedback, and meditation. These techniques are very useful in reducing stress by teaching you how to "rest your mind." In addition, Assertiveness training is often helpful, as is general psychological counseling (such as Cognitive Therapy).

Places where you might find an experienced counselor: Referral from your doctor, your church, local hospital, community mental health program, or local college health service.

ASK YOUR DOCTOR TO PRESCRIBE A "BRAIN CHEMICAL RE-BALANCER"

If, try as you might, you can not lower your stress levels enough to feel well, and if your doctor has found no hidden illness, then you might benefit from the use of a "brain chemical re-balancer". Over the last ten years, a type of medicine has been developed which is not a sleeping pill – – yet it will help you sleep. It is not a stimulant – – yet it will give you energy. It is not a pain reliever – – yet it will diminish aches and increase your enjoyment of life. This family of non-addictive, prescription medicines works by re-balancing your brain's chemical messages.

Now, at this point you may be thinking, "But, Dr. Burns, you have pointed out the dangers of Pick-Me-Up's and Put-Me-Down's, how can you now recommend that we use a medication?" The answer is that these new brain chemical re-balancers, unlike the Pick-Me-Up's and Put-Me-Down's that we have mentioned, do not cause rebound (you don't have a quick upswing followed by a big crash), nor does one develop tolerance to them (you don't have to take more and more just to achieve the desired effect). They can be used to boost your Happy Messengers while you are in the process of lowering your stress load. And, if you are one of the persons who has inherited a very low stress tolerance, you may safely stay on these medications for a very long time.

You can view these medications the way we view insulin for the diabetic. The type I diabetic does not make enough insulin, so he has to take insulin as a long term replacement medicine. If you have lowered your stress levels as much as you can, and if you have no hidden physical illness that is adding hidden stress to your life, and if you are still suffering from OVERSTRESS, you just may be an individual whose genetic inheritance does not allow you to make enough Happy Messengers to meet the basic demands of everyday life. You may indeed benefit from taking these brain chemical re-balancers as a long term replacement medicine.

At present, there are quite a few of these medications that doctors can prescribe. Among these are Amitriptyline,

Nortriptyline, Imipramine, Desipramine, Clomipramine, Doxepin, Trazadone, and Fluoxetine (these are the generic names). Some boost all the Happy Messengers, others boost Serotonin more than Dopamine or Noradrenalin. These re-balancers will help you to sleep well, feel refreshed, and enjoy life. All the medicines have some side effects, but usually your doctor can help you select one that has very little in the way of side effects. (Usually the brain chemical re-balancers have much less side effects than the Pick-Me-Up's and Put-Me-Down's you may be presently using!)

To illustrate the way one uses these re-balancers, I will describe the use of Amitriptyline. Amitriptyline boosts all the Happy Messengers. (Brain chemical re-balancers must be prescribed by a physician after a careful medical history and physical examination. PLEASE do not start or stop any prescription medicine without consulting your physician).

Amitriptyline comes in a 25 mg. pill. Most people should take one, two, or three pills of Amitriptyline, all together at bedtime. Each person requires a slightly different dose of Amitriptyline. Here is how to determine which dose is right for you.

The first night you take one Amitriptyline at bedtime. If you have at least five to six hours of sound sleep and feel rested in the morning, then the dose needed to rebalance your brain chemistry is ONE Amitriptyline pill at bedtime.

If you do not have at least five to six hours sound sleep, increase your dose to two Amitriptyline the following night. If this gives you a restful sleep, then the dose necessary to balance your brain chemistry is TWO Amitriptyline at bedtime.

If two does not result in a restful sleep, then the next night take THREE at bedtime. Whether you need one, two, or three depends on how badly out of balance your brain messengers are. Obviously, the more you can reduce your stress load, the less Amitriptyline you will need to re-balance your brain chemistry.

PRECAUTIONS IN THE USE OF AMITRIPTYLINE

Most people will feel somewhat DROWSY, or slowed down THE FIRST WEEK that they are on Amitriptyline. THIS WILL PASS. But be careful when you drive a car, or operate machinery during this first week. From our discussion of shift work and jet lag, you will recall that it takes about three weeks to reset body rhythms. While they are resetting, you may feel somewhat lethargic. This is why we have you take the Amitriptyline at bedtime. After your body rhythms are reset, the Amitriptyline no longer causes drowsiness, but it continues to help keep your brain chemistry in balance.

By the way, if you are taking TOO MUCH Amitriptyline, you may have a very dry mouth, blurred vision, difficulty starting your urine stream, or rapid heartbeat. The very elderly may become confused. If any of these symptoms do occur, decrease your dosage and tell your doctor right away.

Amitriptyline should not be used if you have a seizure disorder, glaucoma, certain heart diseases or thyroid disease. IF YOU ARE PREGNANT, OR LIKELY TO BECOME PREGNANT while taking the Amitriptyline, do not take the Amitriptyline. It is not known if Amitriptyline, taken during pregnancy, causes adverse effects.

Checklist for
HANDLING
OVERSTRESS

REDUCE YOUR STRESS LOAD:
- ☐ Reduce the pace of change in your life.
- ☐ Reduce social obligations.
- ☐ Reduce work or school obligations.
- ☐ Postpone changes in your living situation.
- ☐ Say "No" more often.
- ☐ Eliminate possible food or environmental allergens.
- ☐ Reduce environmental toxins.

GET OFF THE "ROLLER COASTER":
- ☐ Diet:
    Take a multivitamin, mineral, trace element preparation; stabilize your blood sugar; eat more vegetables.
- ☐ Exercise:
    Twenty minutes to two hours, three times a week.
- ☐ Stop Your Pick-Me-Up's *
- ☐ Stop Your Put-Me-Down's **

DO A "REST FOR YOUR MIND" ACTIVITY:

- ☐ Exercise
- ☐ Recreational reading, arts, crafts, music,
- ☐ Dance
- ☐ Meditation
- ☐ Yoga
- ☐ Biofeedback
- ☐ Self-Hypnosis
- ☐ Religious counseling

HELP YOUR BODY CLOCK RE-SET ITSELF:

- ☐ Set regular sleep times; avoid time zone shifts or rapid changes in your work shift; use daylight spectrum fluorescent lights to set your body clock's "awake time".

VISIT A PHYSICIAN

- ☐ Check for hidden illness **

VISIT A COUNSELOR

- ☐ Obtain help with self relaxation and general psychological counseling.

IF YOU JUST CAN NOT MAKE ENOUGH HAPPY MESSENGER:

- ☐ Use brain chemical re-balancer **

* May need physician supervision to stop heavy intake of Pick-Me-Up's. If in doubt, consult physician.

** Consult physician.

THREE RULES
TO PERMANENTLY
CONQUER
OVERSTRESS

RULE ONE:
LEARN TO READ YOUR BODY SIGNS

Learn to check your body frequently for signs of OVERSTRESS. Watch for the tell-tale disturbances in your sleep pattern, as this is usually the earliest sign of OVER-STRESS.

You must learn to read your body signs in much the same way as the diabetic learns the early warning signs of abnormal blood sugar. In order to cope successfully with diabetes, the diabetic has to learn to read his body's signals. If he has a constant thirst, fatigue and excessive urination, that means the sugar is too high. If he has shakiness, irritability, and perspiration that means the blood sugar is too low. In order to live with diabetes, the diabetic must understand what these signals mean.

Likewise, if you are a person who is prone to OVER-STRESS, you must learn to look for its earliest warning signs. As soon as your sleep patterns change, or you experience fatigue, lack of enjoyment of life, multiple aches and pains – – that is the time to go through the OVERSTRESS checklist.

RULE TWO:
EXCHANGE YOUR STRESSES

Keep your stress level below your individual OVER-STRESS point by "exchanging stresses". If a new stress comes into your life, then make room for it by eliminating or postponing another stress. This way, your TOTAL stress level remains low.

The natural tendency is for people to let their stresses pile up rather than exchanging them. In this fashion, OVER-STRESS gradually occurs. With the development of OVER-STRESS, the person starts using more and more Pick-Me-Up's, taking off on the wild roller coaster of ill health.

IN ORDER TO STAY HEALTHY
LEARN TO EXCHANGE YOUR
STRESSES

RULE THREE:
USE YOUR TOOL BOX

You now have a "TOOL BOX" full of ways to deal with your OVERSTRESS. Whenever your body shows signs of OVERSTRESS, you can use the tools from this book to help set yourself back on the path of well-being.

If you are feeling ill from OVERSTRESS, remember that the troubled sleep, fatigue, aches, lack of enjoyment of life, and even panic attacks are caused by chemical changes in your brain. Effective treatment is available now.

BEGIN TODAY!

10

Epilogue

HERE COMES ANOTHER PLAGUE

Throughout history, mankind has had periodic episodes of illness which have decimated our population. The Bubonic Plague ravaged Europe in the Middle Ages. Syphilis killed one in four Europeans when it was introduced to Europe in the 1500's. Every other Hawaiian was killed by measles in the 1700's. Meanwhile, the Native Americans were slain by smallpox and other imported diseases.

Today, one in ten persons is falling victim to OVER-STRESS. Those who are becoming chemically dependent are walking a fatal path. Others "drop out" at an early age, to join the ranks of society's "marginal survivors".

The cost to society is immense. The effects of OVER-STRESS cost our society at least 60 billion dollars a year. Our society loses through: lost productivity, medical care for the complications of OVERSTRESS, job accidents, and traffic fatalities (half of which are related to driving while using Pick-Me-Up's).

How can it be that one in every ten persons cannot physically adjust to the stress levels found in today's world? The answer lies in our society's pace of CHANGE.

FROM CARRIAGE TO ROCKET SHIP

We certainly live in a society whose hallmark is rapid change. Our broader definition of stress tells us that this rapid change means high stress levels. Most of the human experience on Earth has not involved such a rapid pace of change. Most of the human experience has not prepared us to handle the demands of 20th Century life. That is why one in ten persons is constantly fighting OVERSTRESS.

Let us step outside our present time to see this more clearly. In the state of Utah, near the Great Salt Lake, is an archeological site known as "Danger Cave". Excavation at this site shows a record of human habitation extending back ten thousand years. This record shows that four hundred generations of persons lived basically the same life style and used basically the same tools. Generation upon generation faced similar life conditions, making subtle changes from season to season, and from year to year.

Ways of solving each of life's problems were accumulated in the knowledge of the village elders and religious leaders. This knowledge was then passed from generation to generation. Change, when it did come, occured over millennia.

* A people who hunted with spears learned to use spear throwers to increase their accuracy – – time elapsed: perhaps 5,000 years.

* Bows and arrows greatly increased the accuracy and ease of hunting – – time elapsed: perhaps 4,000 more years.

* Agriculture was developed. In this case, the growing of maize as a crop – – time elapsed: perhaps 2,000 more years.

A future archeological excavation of Salt Lake City would show a gigantic upheaval occuring around 1900 A.D. After ten thousand years of snail-paced change, the future arrived precipitously.

During the course of a single lifetime, a person born in 1900 A.D. has seen the advent of radio, television, computers, automobiles, motocycles, propeller airplanes, jet aircraft, space ships, a moon landing, test tube babies, two wars which involved the entire Earth in conflict, nuclear power generation, and nuclear weapons.

In this environment, the elder generation can no longer be assured of having the "right answer" to every problem. Life is changing radically within the space of even one generation. Today's society has shifted from being elder dominated, where the solutions to life's problems are passed down by the elders, to a "youth culture", where flexibility and adaptability to change are vital if one is to "stay on top of" a continuously changing life. Survival in society today requires more flexibility and adaptability than ever before in human history.

All the preceding years of human existence have not prepared us physically for such a grueling pace of change. One in ten persons is already dropping by the wayside, yet the pace accelerates unabated. Twenty First Century humans will have to maintain physiologic balance in an increasingly stressful sea of technological and cultural changes.

Luckily, an understanding of the problem is emerging which is enabling us to help those with Low Stress Tolerance. As society stress levels continue to rise, we will all need to recognize and counter the effects of – – – OVERSTRESS.

GENERAL REFERENCES FOR FURTHER READING

<u>Physiology of Human Behavior</u>

Biopsychology
John Pinel
Allyn and Bacon, Inc., 1990

The Mind
Richard Restak
Bantum, 1988

Physiology of Behavior, Third Edition
Neil R. Carlson
Allyn and Bacon, Inc., 1986

The Brain
Richard Restak
Bantum, 1985

The Broken Brain
Nancy Andreasen, M.D., Ph.D.
Harper and Row, 1984

<u>Wellness</u>

Wellness Workbook, Second Edition
John. W. Travis, M.D. and Regina Ryan
Ten Speed Press, 1988

The Complete Manual of Fitness and Well-Being
Readers Digest Association, 1984

Nutrition

Nutrition for Living, Second Edition
Janet Christian and Janet Griger
Benjamin Cummings Publishing Co., 1988

Nutrition, Weight Control and Exercise
Frank I. Katch and William McArdle
Lea and Febiger, 1988

Medical Self Help

Taking Care of Yourself
Donald Vickery, M.D. and James Fries, M.D.
Addison Wesley, 1989

BIOGRAPHIES

STEVE BURNS, M.D. is a graduate of U.C.L.A. Medical School. He has been a practicing physician since 1974. Originally trained in Emergency Medicine, his practice for the last decade has been focused upon the issues of Occupational Medicine. He has been the medical consultant for more than four hundred companies in the greater Los Angeles area, helping them deal with issues of worker health and safety. In that time period he has treated over 15,000 individual workers for illness and injury. Dr. Burns is married to Kimberley Burns, and they have a young son.

KIMBERLEY BURNS has been drawing since childhood. While pregnant, Kimberley found that creating cartoons for "Unbearable Stress" was exciting and fun. This is her first book illustration. It is especially noteworthy that Kimberley has had epilepsy all her adult life. She feels it is important that persons with epilepsy know that they can lead normal and very productive lives. Kimberley is currently working on a children's book.

WAYNE NICKENS, M.D., Certified Addiction Medicine Specialist, C.A.C. is a nationally known expert in the field of chemical dependency. He is Past-President of the Foundation for National Education on Alcoholism and Drug Abuse. (A national non-profit educational foundation). His insights into stress and chemical dependency were an important source of ideas for this book. Although he was not able to co-author this book, we wish to thank him for sharing with us his pioneering insights into addiction and stress-related medical illness.

Index